Instant SQL Server Analysis Services 2012 Cube Security

Analyze and secure cubes in the SQL Server 2012 environment in no time using this hands-on guide

Satya SK Jayanty

PUBLISHING

BIRMINGHAM - MUMBAI

Instant SQL Server Analysis Services 2012 Cube Security

First published: July 2013

Production Reference: 1220713

Published by Packt Publishing Ltd.
Livery Place
35 Livery Street
Birmingham B3 2PB, UK.

ISBN 978-1-84968-870-3

www.packtpub.com

Credits

Author
Satya SK Jayanty

Reviewer
Tomislav Piasevoli

Acquisition Editor
Joanne Fitzpatrick

Commissioning Editor
Yogesh Dalvi

Technical Editors
Anita Nayak

Jalasha D'costa

Project Coordinator
Michelle Quadros

Proofreader
Stephen Copestake

Production Coordinator
Aparna Bhagat

Cover Work
Aparna Bhagat

Cover Image
Sheetal Aute

About the Author

Satya (SQLMaster) SK Jayanty is a subject matter expert (Technical & Data Architect and DBA) having more than 21 years of experience in the IT field, which includes a wide range of industries: the Stock Exchange, insurance, telecommunications, financial, retail, and manufacturing sectors, among others.

He has been the Microsoft Most Valuable Professional (MVP) for Architecture – SQL Server since the year 2006.

He has also authored the book *Microsoft SQL Server 2008 R2 Administration Cookbook* (May 2011), *Packt Publishing*. He has co-authored the book *MVP Deep Dives Volume II – SQL Server* (October 2011), *Manning Publications*.

Satya has technically reviewed and provided forewords for three books related to High Availability and Disaster Recovery. And has also been the Item Writer and Technical Reviewer for SQL Server 2008, 2008 R2 and 2012 Microsoft ITPRO and DEV certification exams.

Satya is a regular speaker and SME volunteer at major technology conferences such as Microsoft Tech-Ed (Europe, India, and North America), SQL PASS (Europe and North America), and SQL Bits – the UK and Scottish Area SQL Server user group based in Scotland.

He works as a Director, and Principal Architect, at D B I A Solutions Limited, Database Business Intelligence Architecture Solutions Europe Limited.

First and foremost, I would like to thank my wife Hima for keeping up with me during the writing of this book, particularly as most of the book-writing work occurred on weekends, nights, and other times inconvenient to my family.

Not to mention, my wonderful kids Abhi and Anjali for having patience with me and letting me take another challenge, which has reduced the amount of time I could spend with them.

Finally, a special thanks to Michelle Quadros for supporting me all along in this project.

About the Reviewer

Tomislav Piasevoli is a Business Intelligence (BI) Specialist with a decade of experience working with SQL Server Analysis Services (SSAS). He successfully implemented many still-in-use BI solutions, achieved the highest certification for SQL Server Analysis Services (SSAS Maestro), and shared his expertise in the form of a book named *MDX with SQL Server 2008 R2 Analysis Services Cookbook* published in 2011 by *Packt Publishing* (http://www.amazon.com/dp/1849681309). Tomislav currently specializes in dimensional modeling, cube design, and MDX consulting worldwide and can be contacted at tomislav@piasevoli.com.

In addition to his regular work, Tomislav also finds the time to present at local conferences and to occasionally write an article or two for local magazines or on his blog (http://tomislav.piasevoli.com). His contribution to the community has been recognized by Microsoft honoring him with the Most Valuable Professional (MVP) award every year since 2009.

www.PacktPub.com

Support files, eBooks, discount offers and more

You might want to visit www.PacktPub.com for support files and downloads related to your book.

Did you know that Packt offers eBook versions of every book published, with PDF and ePub files available? You can upgrade to the eBook version at www.PacktPub.com and as a print book customer, you are entitled to a discount on the eBook copy. Get in touch with us at service@packtpub.com for more details.

At www.PacktPub.com, you can also read a collection of free technical articles, sign up for a range of free newsletters and receive exclusive discounts and offers on Packt books and eBooks.

http://PacktLib.PacktPub.com

Do you need instant solutions to your IT questions? PacktLib is Packt's online digital book library. Here, you can access, read and search across Packt's entire library of books.

Why Subscribe?

- ▶ Fully searchable across every book published by Packt
- ▶ Copy and paste, print and bookmark content
- ▶ On demand and accessible via web browser

Free Access for Packt account holders

If you have an account with Packt at www.PacktPub.com, you can use this to access PacktLib today and view nine entirely free books. Simply use your login credentials for immediate access.

Table of Contents

Preface

Welcome to *Instant SQL Server Analysis Services 2012 Cube Security*. You must know that a broad range of activities, such as building solutions and deploying analytical databases for Business Intelligence (BI), is contained within a Cube. SQL Server 2012 Analysis Services provides a wide range of solutions within BI with Excel, Performance Point, Reporting Services, and SharePoint services. The BI semantics from SQL Server 2012 Analysis Services requires robust security and protection for analytics to manage the Cube data. This book covers the key steps in security and highlights the required model along with connecting relational data for processing.

What this book covers

Designing and creating security roles in an OLAP database (Intermediate) begins with security management with a design and creates phases that are initial steps to defining the security roles, irrespective of relational database type or analytical database type.

Creating security roles (Intermediate) covers the topic where, in order to manage security for Analysis Services objects and data, a role is important. This associates relevant operating system security identifiers that will build a much more robust system.

Defining dimension access privileges (Advanced) will look through dimension access privileges. As an administrator, your responsibility is to grant relevant read or write permissions to some or all members of any dimension in the cubes to which the database role has access permissions.

Managing role-based security – database to cube level (Advanced) will look at how to grant access and permissions from the database to cube level within an Analysis Services database.

Managing role-based security – dimension to cell level (Advanced) will look through how to grant access and permissions from the dimension to cell level within an Analysis Services database.

Accessing restrictions on dimensions and defining default members – full and partial (Intermediate) lets us overview access restrictions and define the default members with necessary permissions.

Securing data at the cell level (Intermediate) will look through the key steps in securing data at the cell level within a cube.

Preventing read/access to cell data (Intermediate) highlights the essential steps to limit the cell data access within the cube or dimension that will explicitly restrict cell access.

Managing user-access privileges on a cube (Advanced) will look through the user-access privileges on the cube.

Managing security roles for processing (Intermediate) explains the important security roles that are essential for cube processing.

Data source and access control on cubes (Advanced) will go through the key aspects on how the access control can be affected to the data sources and dimension data that are included in the cube.

Building secure BI platform – the journey from SQL Server 2008 R2 to 2012 (Intermediate) provides an explanation of what it takes to build a secure BI platform with highlights on enhancements to the product while transitioning from SQL Server 2008 R2 to 2012. In this recipe, we will go through the important aspects in building a secure BI platform on the instance level along with enhancements that are incorporated in SQL Server since version 2008 R2.

Securing key points in SSAS (Advanced) provides an addition to the previous recipe on securing the key points within a SSAS instance that are associated outside of the SQL Server instance.

What you need for this book

In order to fulfill the criteria, we need the following prerequisites for the book:

- ▶ SQL Server 2012 Management Studio (SSMS).
- ▶ The AdventureWorks2012 database. We can obtain the necessary database files and database product samples from SQL Server Database Product Samples landing page at `http://msftdbprodsamples.codeplex.com/releases/view/55330`

 These sample databases cannot be installed on any version of SQL Server other than SQL Server 2012 RTM and higher.

- ▶ Ensure that you install the databases to your specified 2012 version instance.
- ▶ A new OLAP database using this script `AdventureWorksDM.xmla` file.

Who this book is for

This book is aimed at helping the key people in the data platform administration and management world, such as Data Architects, Developers, and Aspiring Database Administrators.

Conventions

In this book, you will find a number of styles of text that distinguish between different kinds of information. Here are some examples of these styles, and an explanation of their meaning.

Code words in text are shown as follows: "A full set of properties can also be found in the `msmdsrv.ini` file."

New terms and **important words** are shown in bold. Words that you see on the screen, in menus or dialog boxes for example, appear in the text like this: "Click on the **Dimensions** option in the **Select a Page** pane."

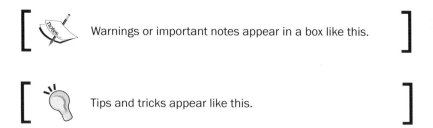

Warnings or important notes appear in a box like this.

Tips and tricks appear like this.

Reader feedback

Feedback from our readers is always welcome. Let us know what you think about this book—what you liked or may have disliked. Reader feedback is important for us to develop titles that you really get the most out of.

To send us general feedback, simply send an e-mail to `feedback@packtpub.com`, and mention the book title via the subject of your message.

If there is a topic that you have expertise in and you are interested in either writing or contributing to a book, see our author guide on `www.packtpub.com/authors`.

Customer support

Now that you are the proud owner of a Packt book, we have a number of things to help you to get the most from your purchase.

Downloading the example code

You can download the example code files for all Packt books you have purchased from your account at `http://www.packtpub.com`. If you purchased this book elsewhere, you can visit `http://www.packtpub.com/support` and register to have the files e-mailed directly to you.

Errata

Although we have taken every care to ensure the accuracy of our content, mistakes do happen. If you find a mistake in one of our books—maybe a mistake in the text or the code—we would be grateful if you would report this to us. By doing so, you can save other readers from frustration and help us improve subsequent versions of this book. If you find any errata, please report them by visiting `http://www.packtpub.com/submit-errata`, selecting your book, clicking on the **errata submission form** link, and entering the details of your errata. Once your errata are verified, your submission will be accepted and the errata will be uploaded on our website, or added to any list of existing errata, under the Errata section of that title. Any existing errata can be viewed by selecting your title from `http://www.packtpub.com/support`.

Piracy

Piracy of copyright material on the Internet is an ongoing problem across all media. At Packt, we take the protection of our copyright and licenses very seriously. If you come across any illegal copies of our works, in any form, on the Internet, please provide us with the location address or website name immediately so that we can pursue a remedy.

Please contact us at `copyright@packtpub.com` with a link to the suspected pirated material.

We appreciate your help in protecting our authors, and our ability to bring you valuable content.

Questions

You can contact us at `questions@packtpub.com` if you are having a problem with any aspect of the book, and we will do our best to address it.

Instant SQL Server Analysis Services 2012 Cube Security

Welcome to *Instant SQL Server Analysis Services 2012 Cube Security*.

The launch of Microsoft SQL Server 2012 brings a new edition called **Business Intelligence** (**BI**). This edition joins the SQL Server family, which can be classified as a milestone release from Microsoft Corporation.

In the current real-world scenario, the underlying hardware such as disk speed, memory, and processing power have no limits to completely guarantee acceptable levels of performance from a database or SQL Server instance. Similarly, the features from the 2012 version are also high-end to keep up the performance, scalability, and availability of the data platform.

Since the inception of SQL Server 2008, security has become the paramount feature, which is implemented by default. This kind of authorization is intended to support the organizations that nonexistence of skilled DBAs, to securely deploy the SQL Server features. The compliance and regulations within the financial industry have elevated Microsoft's responsibility to provide a baseline functionality to deliver the true scale of security and manageability features.

Then, coming to the data access layer, the highlight within the security method is **Transparent Data Encryption** (**TDE**) to protect data and **Extensible Key Management** (**EKM**) to enable accessibility to the protected data in the form of a key password. The Windows operating system (and not only in the SQL Server arena) has also contributed authentication features, such as Kerberos Authentication that will accomplish robust authentication methods to access the data platform. SQL Server 2012 continues with similar levels of security features: secure by design, secure by default, and secure in deployment.

In practice, **SQL Server Analysis Services** (**SSAS**) is just a part of the Business Intelligence (BI) tool that provides next-generation data warehousing capabilities. To conform to a complete SQL Server BI platform, services such as core-database engine, **SQL Server Reporting Services** (**SSRS**), and **SQL Server Integration Services** (**SSIS**) are essential.

BI solutions comprise key findings that detail data and trend analysis that require data integration, cleansing, and transformation. Right on time with the current social networking plugins such as Facebook, Twitter, LinkedIn, and MySpace, they add more fuel to the fire that leads to the data explosion.

Similarly, the need of data usage from mainframe computer to the mobile devices, it is the data flow that keeps the business running. The primary concern with such vast amounts of data flow across multiple systems, the BI helps business to make strategic decisions at the right time. This is where security becomes a prime concern when the data leaves the corporate network and it must be presented to the right owner without compromise or any data leaks.

With regard to trustworthy computing concepts, it is over 10 years now since security features were developed and enhanced from version to version. Here are a few of the best security features (my favorite) that are built-in within SQL Server as compared to other RDBMS products:

- ▶ Server scope roles and database-specific roles enabling user-defined roles
- ▶ Compliance and resiliency while using auditing features
- ▶ Providing a default schema for groups to simplify security
- ▶ SQL Server 2012 offers contained database authentication, which as the name suggests provides authentication without any need for server logins
- ▶ Windows Authentication and password policies for SQL logins
- ▶ Higher security within end user reports that are originated from SharePoint, Microsoft Dynamics, and Exchange

This chapter covers the recipes that are a foundation to security and its importance within SSAS on **Online Analytical Process** (**OLAP**) databases, which are essential for an organization to disperse the data effectively without compromising the confidentiality of data.

Security in particular for an **Analysis Services** platform is an important issue that needs to be properly administered and managed. As this book relates to the cube, it is an important subject that needs to be highlighted. A cube contains data for a particular dataset or a whole organization. Specific to the subset of data as a DBA, you need to ensure that such data can only be accessed by relevant privileged people in the organization.

Nevertheless, security is paramount for a data platform; it can be fixed in the initial stages of design that will certainly avoid any breach of data access layers. So the recipes from this chapter consist of the required ingredients to construct and administer OLAP security management:

- Designing and creating security roles in OLAP database
- Creating security roles
- Defining dimension access privileges

By the time this book was written, SQL Server 2012 Service Pack 1 was released, so the majority of the SSAS features information that are referred here are applicable for RTM + Service Pack 1 releases.

The introduction of **Business Intelligence Semantic Model** (**BISM**) facilitates and supports a wide range of reporting and analytics while blending the two Analysis Services modeling features: Multidimensional and Tabular.

- Multidimensional modeling, a part of SQL Server OLAP services since version 7.0, enables users to create multidimensional cubes composed of measures and dimensions based on data contained in a relational database using traditional OLAP.
- Tabular modeling offers self-serviced data modeling experience. This model organizes data into related tables that require Analysis Services configuration to operate in tabular mode.

 It is essential to stress that tabular model is not a replacement for multidimensional model, but is a supplement it.

Specific to the Business Intelligence arena we have a new feature called tabular modeling. This is a new addition for the Business Analysts that can build up a BI semantic model using the relational tables from the database engine rather than using the dimensions from Analysis Services.

This BI edition contains a majority of Enterprise edition's data management features, such as **Master Data Services** (**MDS**), **Data Quality Services** (**DQS**), **Power Pivot**, and **Manageability**. As the name suggests, the majority of the features for Corporate BI are also in-the-box such as CUBE analytics, Reporting related features, Multidimensional BI Semantic model, Self-service Business Intelligence, Alerting, and Power Pivot for SharePoint Server.

As a Database Administrator and Data Architect the data security is a prime concern and this book spotlights the key concepts on securing the CUBE. So we need to understand the SQL Server security model and how to effectively implement the same on the data platform. Simply, security does not mean stopping at delegating access control on server-scope to column-level or defining a strong password for a SQL user.

The Administration and Management to data platform relies upon Manageability enhancements, so it is essential to contain appropriate tools to manage the SQL Server data platform.

SQL Server Management Studio (**SSMS**) is the key resource in Manageability aspects that has been introduced in version 2005 and became popular since version 2008 with greater enhancements. It's not just that the SSMS is being used by DBAs & Developers; with SQL Server 2012 the manageability enhancement augments the developer's working experience with the product.

Similarly, just to leverage policy-based management, resource governor or managing SQL Server scheduled jobs, SSMS can be used to debug the code using Transact-SQL (TSQL) debugger, IntelliSense enhancements that suggest string matches based on selective words. Also, the newest addition within SSMS is the Insert Snippet menu that allows developers to insert a template as a reference when writing TSQL statements.

Business Intelligence Development Studio (**BIDS**) is the one tool that delivers the BI development capabilities for Analysis Services, Reporting Services, and Integration Services, which is versions 2008 and 2008 R2.

Combining together the SSMS and BIDS provides the tools for data platform administration, security, and all required management functions.

The BIDS is a unique tool to perform views, charts, and prediction-analysis in addition to the free-form query editor to build ad hoc **Data Mining Extensions** (**DMX**) queries to manage the data mining models in Analysis Services.

Designing and creating security roles in an OLAP database (Intermediate)

Designing and creating are the initial steps to define the security roles, irrespective of the type of database, whether it is a relational-database or analytical-database.

A primary reflection of security roles in a database highlights the behavioral changes of users and schemas separation since SQL Server 2005 version.

In a relational world, schemas are no longer equivalent to database users (they are simply a container of objects) and each schema has a distinct namespace that exists independently of the database user who created it. Such separation enables the administrators to grant necessary privileges on schemas to the corresponding database users.

Similarly, security roles also play very important role in the SSAS world. To manage security for Analysis Services objects and data, a role can be associated to the **Security Identifiers** (let us refer to them as SIDs) of Windows operating system users and groups that have specific access rights and permissions defined for the objects managed by SSAS instance.

Let us see how to construct security management and fulfill security roles criteria from the first recipe in this instant cookbook.

Getting ready

In order to fulfill the criteria we need the following prerequisites and steps:

- ▸ SQL Server 2012 Management Studio (SSMS)
- ▸ AdventureWorks2012 database: we can obtain the necessary database files and database product samples from SQL Server Database Product Samples downloads page `http://msftdbprodsamples.codeplex.com/releases/view/55330`.

 These sample databases cannot be installed on any version of SQL Server other than SQL Server 2012 RTM or higher.

- ▸ Ensure you install the databases to your specified 2012 version instance
- ▸ For the sake of this book I have created a new OLAP database using the `AdventureWorksDM.xmla` script file

How to do it...

In order to create security it is essential to create a Windows user and group that will enable the remaining recipes in this book to proceed. Here we will browse through the Windows Server 2008 R2 operating system options.

Once the prerequisites mentioned in the preceding *Getting ready* section are completed, follow these steps:

1. Navigate to **Start | Control Panel** and choose **Administrative Tools**, then open the **Computer Management (Local)** program.
2. Expand the `Local Users` and `Groups` folder.
3. Right-click on **Users** to create a new user. For the sake of this recipe I have created a user named `DBIA_BI_User`.
4. Right-click on **Groups** to create a new group, name the group as `BI_User`, add the newly created user **DBIA_BI_User,** and click on **OK**.

5. To relate to the preceding steps you should have similar properties shown as per the following screenshot:

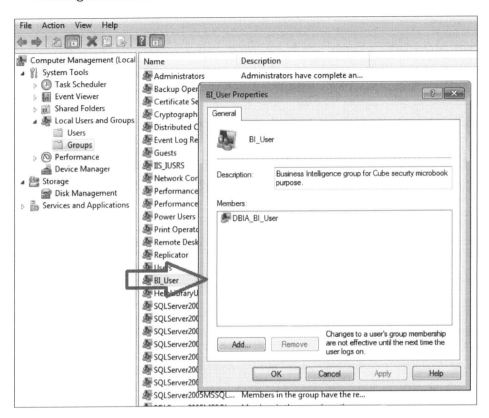

6. Now the initial requirement of a local user and group on the server is completed, let us jump into SQL Server Management Studio that is specific to Analysis Services instance security.

7. Open the SSMS and choose **Connect to Analysis Services...** (AS) instance.

8. Right-click on the selected AS instance and choose **Properties**.

9. Within that **Properties** page select the **Security** option that will show the default **Server administrators**.

Further we can choose the corresponding local or domain group to be part of the **Server Administrators** role. For the purpose of this recipe we can skip the option of adding any additional group at this moment.

How it works...

The preceding steps will be the starter steps to design and create security roles in an OLAP database.

The steps to create a specific security role within the analytical database area needs elaboration, as it is different from the Server role and the Database role from the relational database world. Similarly, security roles also play a very important role in the SSAS world. To manage security for Analysis Services objects and data, a role can be associated to the SIDs of Windows operating system users and groups that have specific access rights and permissions defined for the objects managed by SSAS instance.

The Analysis Services instance property pages from SSMS will show (and contain) a subset of properties (by default) that are likely to be modified. In order to obtain a full set of properties, click on the **Show Advanced (All) Properties** checkbox at the bottom of the server properties page. Similarly, a full set of properties can also be found in the `msmdsrv.ini` file.

Creating security roles (Intermediate)

To manage security for Analysis Services objects and data, a role is important that associates relevant SIDs of the operating system that will build much more robust system. The Windows users and groups that have specific rights and privileges defined can be incorporated in Analysis Services. There are two different types of roles:

- ▶ **Server role**: This is a fixed role for administrator access to Analysis Services instance
- ▶ **Database roles**: These are defined by the administrators to manage access to objects and data for users (non-administrator users)

Getting ready

To explain the topic further, a role is a containing object for a collection of users that are classified as members. In this recipe we will overview the steps in creating security roles within Analysis Services database.

The prerequisite for this recipe can be obtained from the *Getting ready* section in the *Designing and creating security roles in an OLAP Database* recipe.

How to do it...

Once the above prerequisites are completed follow the steps below:

1. Open the SSMS and choose **Connect to Analysis Services...** instance.
2. Expand SQL Server 2012 instance and the **Databases** folder.

3. Choose the database **AdventureWorksDM** (created within the *Getting Ready* section from the *Designing and creating security roles in an OLAP Database* recipe) and expand the **Roles** folder.

4. Right-click on the **Roles** folder to create a new role:

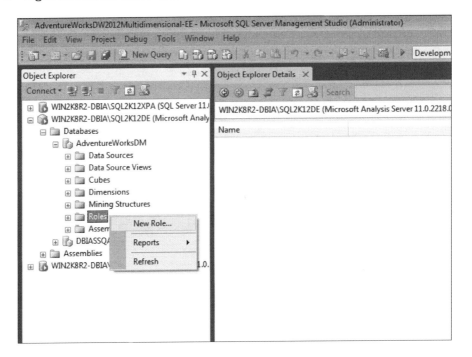

Until SQL Server 2008 R2, a new role could be created by attempting to right-click on the **Role** node within the **Solution Explorer** pane within Business Intelligence Development Studio (BIDS) too. However BIDS tool is deprecated from SQL Server 2012.

To manage and administer the BI technologies, Analysis Services, Integration Services, and Reporting Services, use SQL Server Management Studio tool, which is associated with each of these technologies and is slightly different.

5. Choose the name of this New Role as `DBIA_Reader` and opt for **Read definition** (as seen in the following screenshot).

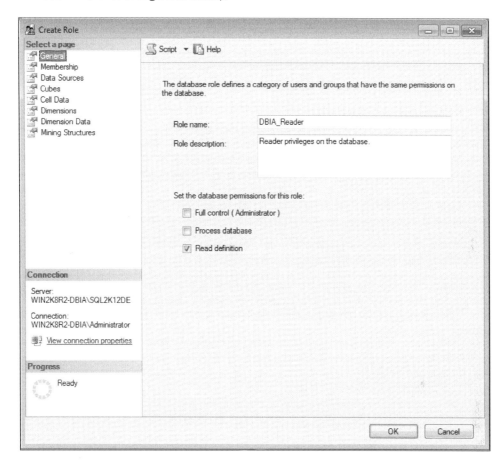

6. The remaining vertical screen-tab options from the **Select a page** option are explained as follows:

    ❑ **General**: The best place to highlight which role is defined for the selected Analysis Services database.

    ❑ **Membership**: Choose the corresponding local and domain users/groups to be added for this role.

    ❑ **Data Sources**: An essential place to use data mining functionality within Analysis Services. (Unless we have created Data Sources on SSMS Object Explorer, the Data Source screen area will be blank).

    ❑ **Cubes**: A place to set up several cube-level permissions (right to access and administrative).

    ❑   **Cell Data**: To define security at the cell level within the cube; this is relevant only when the corresponding **Cubes** option is defined in the preceding option.

    ❑   **Dimensions**: This is relevant for all database dimensions level permissions.

    ❑   **Dimension Data**: The security that allows Basic and Advanced options for Attributes Hierarchy. You can select or de select all members along with Allowed, Denied and Default member sets.

7. Once the relevant options are set click on **OK** to create the specified role within the Analysis Services database.

As you may have observed that the preceding steps confirm the creation of the **Reader** privileged role, for the sake of multiple recipes specific to Security Roles let us create two additional roles that will be different to each other on the AS database.

Follow these steps for creating two additional roles that will be different to each other on the AS database

1. Choose the name of this new role as `DBIA_User`.

2. Click on **OK** to create the specified role within the Analysis Services database.

3. Choose the name of this New Role as `DBIA_Processor` and opt for the **Process database** permission under the **Set the database permissions for this role** option. (see the preceding screenshot for more information).

4. Click on **OK** to create the specified role within the Analysis Services database.

How it works...

The preceding steps enable us to create the necessary security roles that are essential to manage security in Analysis Services objects and data.

The steps to create a specific security role within analytical databases needs elaboration, as it is different from the Server role and the Database role from the relational database world. Similarly, security roles also play very important roles in the SSAS world.

To manage security for Analysis Services objects and data, a role can be associated to the SIDs of Windows operating system users and groups that have specific access rights and permissions defined for the objects managed by SSAS instance.

The two different types of permissions that can be granted to a user are classified as Administrative Security and Data Security. Again such a level of permissions varies from the object of an Analysis Services Database. For instance a user can be granted to execute Local Cube read permissions on the Data Security level and Read Definition on the Administrative Security level.

Security is managed by using roles and permissions. Roles are groups of users and users can be referred to as members. Such members can be added or removed from the roles.

Permissions that are specified by roles can use the objects for which that role has permissions, as they apply to all the members in a role who have equal permissions to the objects. Also, the `permissions` collection of the object has a single role assigned to it.

Defining dimension access privileges (Advanced)

A **dimension** is the key factor within Analysis Services database that consists of a list of attributes that will be used to analyze data. For instance, an attribute of customers may be represented by their sales volume or geographical area.

Whenever we build an Analysis Services solution the AS dimension objects are built from the dimension tables. The dimensional architecture keeps the Analysis Services database intact to provide Business Intelligence features.

Getting ready

In this recipe we will overview the dimension access privileges. As an administrator your responsibility is to grant relevant read or write permissions to some or all the members of any dimension in the cubes to which the database role has access permissions.

The prerequisite for this recipe can be obtained from the *Getting ready* section in the *Designing and creating security roles in an OLAP database* recipe.

How to do it...

Once the prerequisites are completed follow the following steps:

1. Open the SSMS and choose the **Connect to Analysis Services...** instance.
2. Expand SQL Server 2012 instance and the **Databases** folder.
3. Choose the appropriate database `AdventureWorksDM` (that was created within the preceding *Getting ready* section) and expand the **Roles** folder.

As the `AdventureWorksDM` database is created with pre-existing Data Sources, Data Source Views, and Dimensions, we will have an opportunity to view the relevant Dimensions on the following screens:

> ► In conjunction with the *Creating security roles (Intermediate)* recipe we have already created three roles on `AdventureWorksDM` database, named as `DBIA_Reader`, `DBIA_Processor`, and `DBIA_User`.

As per the their naming convention the `DBIA_Reader` role has read access on the database that will automatically impersonate Read Definition privilege for the users that are associated within this role.

Similarly, the `DBIA_Processor` has been granted a Process Database privilege that will automatically impersonate Process privileges for the users that are associated within this role.

4. Expand the **Roles** folder and right-click on the **DBIA_User** role to choose **Properties**.

5. Click on the **Dimensions** option in the **Select a Page** pane (left-hand side).

6. Now locate the dimension in the **Select Dimension Set** and ensure that the **All database dimensions** option is selected from the drop-down list.

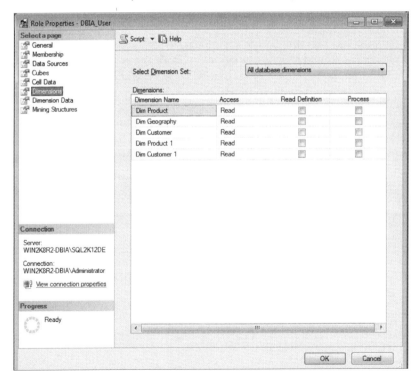

See the preceding screenshot that displays the relevant privileges for the role **DBIA_User**.

7. As there were permissions set for the role **DBIA_user** role under the **Set the database permissions for this role** option all the corresponding **Read Definition and Process** checkboxes are blank.

8. Now, on this screen, click on the **Read Definition** checkbox against the **Dim Product** and **Dim Product1** dimension names.

9. Further choose the **Process** checkbox for the **Dim Geography** dimension name.

10. Click on **OK** to apply the corresponding changes in this recipe.

In addition to specifying the read (**Read Definition**) or read/write (**Process**) dimension access privileges to a database role, we can define specific attribute hierarchies and members within the dimension to which role members are allowed access by choosing the **Dimension Data** option under the **Select a page** option on the left-hand pane.

How it works...

In this recipe and the previous one (*Creating security roles*) we have performed the necessary steps to create security roles and granted required privileges for these roles.

To re-iterate what follows from the preceding steps, we have already created three roles on `AdventureWorksDM` database, named as **DBIA_Reader**, **DBIA_Processor**, and **DBIA_User**.

As per the their naming convention the DBIA_Reader role has read access on the database that will automatically impersonate the Read Definition privilege for the users that are associated within this role.

Similarly, the DBIA_Processor has been granted with Process Database privilege that will automatically impersonate Process privileges for the users that are associated within this role.

According to Microsoft documentation,

> Since the SQL Server 2005 Analysis Services (SSAS) design concept, by default a database role in Analysis Services database has read permissions on all dimension members in each cube to which the database role has access permissions.

SSAS relies on Windows operating system authentication methods to authenticate users.

This means by default only authenticated users who have rights can establish the connection to the Analysis Services instance. The access privileges are determined by the rights that are assigned on instance level and database level. This process will work directly from the Windows operating system or through the membership in the Windows role.

- ▶ The Server Administrator role is a single fixed-server role that grants relevant member permission to perform any task within the Analysis Services instance
- ▶ Each database role has a customized set of permission to let the users access data or perform tasks within a database, dimension, or cube

Multiple privileges such as read and/or process can be granted to each role within the AS database. A database role can specify whether the associated members have permission to view or update members in specified database dimensions.

Similarly, on a cube level that is based on a single-database dimension will have multiple cube dimensions defined. The permissions that are specified for the database dimensions apply to all the cube dimensions unless these permissions are overridden for one or more of the cube dimensions.

There's more...

By default, members with at least read access to an attribute member have read access to all cube cells related to the attribute member. You can limit cell access to specific cells. We will overview this topic under the *Securing data at the cell level (Intermediate)* recipe.

As we have cooked through a few recipes from the basics to construct the administer OLAP security management, the recipes associated in this security essentials will cruise through dimension to cell level within an OLAP database.

By default the best practices (and Microsoft) recommend to use Windows authentication based security. In some occasions this may not be possible by design or due to some architectural restrictions where the integrated security feature is used. Irrespective of either authentication methods it is highly recommended to use account credentials to access the data on database.

An authentication and access privilege brings up an impersonation topic that works seamlessly from the database level down to the cell level. In this book the recipes will highlight the role-based security from dimension to cell level and database to cube level. Also, covered are the features surrounding how to restrict access to dimensions and define default members (full and partial).

The following recipes will go through the security aspects on dimension level, how we can specify whether its members have permissions to view or update dimension members in a specific database dimension. For instance, a database role is not granted permissions to view or update a particular dimension. In this case some or all of the dimension's members of the database have no permission to view the dimensions of any of its members.

Similarly to the cells level a database role can specify whether its members have read, read contingent, or process permission on some or all of the cells within a cube. On the contrary, if a database role is granted permission to view members of a dimension, cell-level security can be used to limit these cell members from the dimension that the database role members can view.

In managing role-based security the two recipes *Managing role-based security – dimension to cell level (Advanced)* and *Managing role based security – database to cube level (Advanced)* are inter-related. In order to accomplish these tasks we will perform the steps as a two-fold process. Initially we will work upon database to cube level based security that will enable us to perform dimension to cell level steps.

Managing role-based security – database to cube level (Advanced)

In OLAP, within the Analysis Services database the cube plays an important role to provide Business Intelligence to the end users. A cube is represented as a multi dimensional structure that contains data used for analytical purposes. In this regard, the main pillars for the cube are dimensions and measures. Dimensions highlight structure and measures provide aggregated values for calculation.

In a logical design a cube allows the end users or client application to retrieve values of measures. These are contained in cells in the cube, cells represent summarized values that are referred as measures too.

Talking about cube permissions within SSAS, a database role has no permissions to view any cubes in the database. In order to obtain the necessary database that database role can be granted relevant permissions to a cube that will be transformed to cell level too.

In this recipe we will see how to grant access and permissions from database to cube level within an Analysis Services database.

 The prerequisite for this recipe can be obtained from the *Getting ready* section from the *Designing and creating security roles in an OLAP database* recipe.

How to do it...

Once the above prerequisites are completed follow these steps:

1. Open the SSMS and choose the **Connect to Analysis Services...** instance.
2. Expand the SQL Server 2012 instance and the **Databases** folder.
3. Choose the **AdventureWorksDM** database and expand the **Roles** folder.

4. Select the **DBIA_Reader** role and right-click to show **Properties**.

5. Click on **Cubes** in the **Select a page** pane, where the deployed cube will be displayed to grant **Access** and **Local Cube/Drillthrough Access** privileges.

6. Here we will choose both the **Read** option at the **Access** dropdown and the **Drillthrough** option at the **Local Cube/Drillthrough Access** column (see the following screenshot).

7. Do not grant access to the **Process** cube; thus, leave the check box blank.

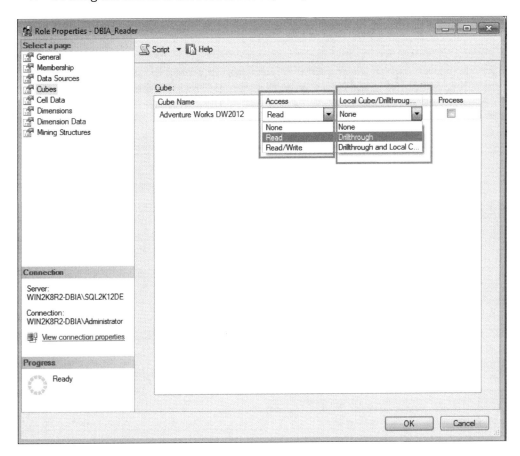

8. Click on **OK** to apply the corresponding changes at this point.

How it works...

The first steps in managing role-based security access to cube level is essential that will in turn enable the process to define cell based access on the Analysis Services database.

The preceding set of steps will grant necessary access privileges to the database roles. However, it is essential to highlight the associated action within the process; the **Drillthrough** option at the **Local Cube/Drillthrough Access** column is classified as an action. This can be termed as an end user-initiated operation upon a selected cube or portion of a cube. As per the settings or code actions, an operation can start another application with the selected item as a parameter or retrieve information about the selected item, which in turn deviates the security policies.

As per the Microsoft documentation the actions are differentiated as three types:

▶ **Drillthrough actions**: These return a set of rows that represents the underlying data of the selected cells of the cube, where the action occurs

▶ **Reporting actions**: These return a report from Reporting Services that is associated with the selected section of the cube, where the action occurs

▶ **Standard actions**: These return the action element (URL, HTML, DataSet, RowSet, and other elements) that is associated with the selected section of the cube, where the action occurs

The Drillthrough action is also used within a mining model, which is termed as when a user browses through the model, they can retrieve detailed information about the cases that were used to create the model. In relevance to this, necessary permissions and the structure must have already been processed.

There's more...

By default the database role, which grants read or write permissions to a cube and all the associated role members, will have relevant access to all cube cells unless permissions are specifically restricted on specific cells.

In order to accomplish such cell-based privileges, or if you want to grant write permission on specific cells in the cube to database role members, you can refer to the following recipe.

Managing role-based security – dimension to cell level (Advanced)

Cubes – an important ingredient in OLAP to provide Business Intelligence to the end users. A cube is composed of cells that are organized by the measure groups and dimensions. On its own, a cell represents the unique logical intersection in a cube.

A cube is represented as a multidimensional structure that contains data used for analytical purpose. In this regard, the main pillars for cube are dimensions and measures. Dimensions highlight the structure and measures provide aggregated values for calculations purposes.

In a logical design, a cube allows end users or a client application to retrieve values of measures. These are contained in cells in the cube. Cells represent summarized values, which are also referred to as measures.

As we talked through previous recipes, in SSAS once a database role is created and granted with read or process permissions to a cube, then role members will have access to view all the cell data. In order to restrict such an action and access to specific cells, we must specifically restrict cell access. Within these cells, certain calculations can be derived using measures, which represent columns that contain data (numeric) that can be aggregated. By default, a measure is mapped to a column, in a fact table.

It is also essential to talk about derived cells access, in addition to a single cell in a cube. For these derived cells, the data is obtained from other cells. For instance, there are three measures (cost, sales, and profit) associated to cells named quarterly, which is used to derive profit on sales for a product. In this case, a database role has permissions on profit and sales measures but not on cost, so it may be possible for a member of that database role to infer the values of cells to which it does not have permissions.

In this recipe we will see how to grant access and permissions from the dimension to cell level within an Analysis Services database.

 The prerequisite for this recipe can be obtained from the *Getting ready* section in the *Designing and creating security roles in an OLAP database* recipe.

How to do it...

Once the prerequisites are completed, perform the following steps:

1. Open the SSMS and choose the **Connect to Analysis Services...** instance.
2. Expand the SQL Server 2012 instance and the `Databases` folder.
3. Choose the **AdventureWorksDM** database (which was created within the *Getting ready* section mentioned) and expand the `Roles` folder.
4. Now, select the **DBIA_Reader** role and right-click to show properties.

5. Choose the **Cell Data** option in the **Select a page** pane, which presents three different types of permissions for the cell data.

6. Let us select the **Enable read-contingent permissions** checkbox for the **DBIA_Reader** role:

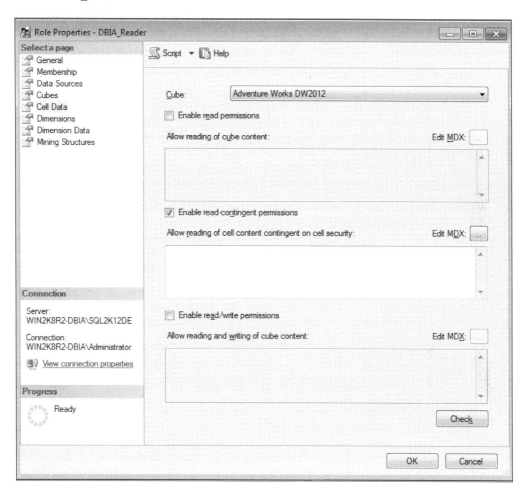

7. Additionally, to grant permissions specifically to certain members enter the relevant MDX expression in the **Allow read of cell content contingent on cell security** box (see the preceding screenshot).

 Also, you can click on the **Edit MDX** button to build the **multidimensional expressions** (**MDX**), which will enable you to build relevant MDX expressions (see the following screenshot). This is useful for users who have experience in using the MDX programming language.

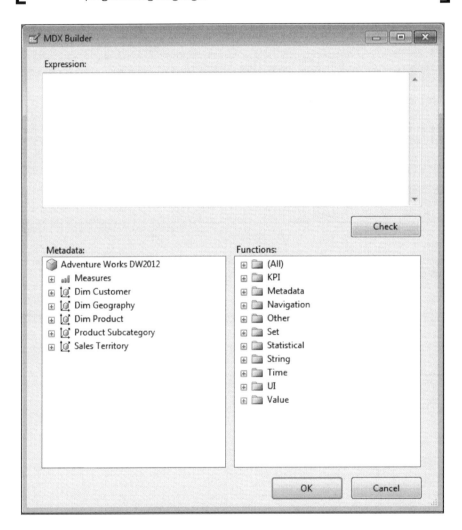

8. Click on **OK** to apply the corresponding changes for the preceding set of steps.

How it works...

As we talked through previous recipes in SSAS, once a database role is created and granted with read or process permissions to a cube, then role members will have access to view all the cell data.

In order to restrict such an action and access to specific cells, we must specifically restrict cell access. Within these cells, certain calculations can be derived using measures, which represent columns that contain data (numeric) that can be aggregated. By default a measure is mapped to a column in a fact table.

The previous steps define the simple process of granting access within a cube for cell data; in additional to these actions a certain level of access can be granted to specific members of a database role.

The flexibility of security provision, by allowing access to cells for specific members in some dimensions and denying access to cells for specific members, is possible as per the previous steps. By default all the members associated in that database role will have relevant privileges on all the cube cells within that cube, if no members are entered. The option within the **Allow reading of cell content contingent on cell security** box inherits such actions of denials. For certain members you can create an MDX expression that allows or denies access to any possible combination of cells.

There's more...

In certain cases, the permissions that are granted on specific cells cannot exceed the permissions associated to a database role on the cube. In this case the permissions that were set on cube level will be used. For instance, a database role has read/write permissions on a cell, but that same role has only read permission on the cube; in that case, the cell data permission will be set to read only.

Although a database role may have access to cell data, that role will not have access to dimension data unless the role has been given read or read/write permissions to the dimension data separately. Access to cube data can restrict access to dimension attributes to which the database role has access, but cannot extend access to dimension attributes to which the database role does not have access.

More information – section 1

Consider you have to grant elevated privileges in addition to read permissions to a role, unless the role has been given read or read/write permissions to the dimension data separately. In such cases, access to cube data can restrict access to dimension attributes to which the database role has access.

Accessing restrictions on dimensions and defining default members – full and partial (Intermediate)

The key part of keeping up the cube security is referred to in the previous recipe, *Managing role-based security – dimension to cell level (Advanced)*.

However, the important aspects on how to restrict access on certain dimensions within the cube are essential as well. In this recipe let us look at the access restrictions and define the default members with necessary permissions. The default members in a database role can also be restricted or be granted access to the dimensions.

The key part of accessing the cube is managed from the dimension to cell level. As a cube is represented as multidimensional structure that contains data used for analytical purposes, the dimensions will always provide a necessary structure for the data presentation, and for the databases roles we need, to secure the necessary grants and permissions.

As the recipe heading specifies, defining default members (full and partial) means granting necessary access to the all dimensions (full) or few dimensions (partial). Since SQL Server 2005, the database roles have the necessary permissions to read or write to the dimensions in a cube. However, with this recipe we will dive into defining access restrictions to a specific set of attribute members for each dimension elements to which role members have necessary permission access (either granted or denied attributes).

 The prerequisite for this recipe can be obtained from the *Getting ready* section in the *Designing and creating security roles in an OLAP database* recipe.

How to do it...

The recipe steps are bifurcated as basic and advanced; this will enable us to grant database role access to a member in the dimension:

1. Start the SQL Server Management Studio and connect to the SQL Server 2012 Analysis Services instance.

2. Expand the `Databases` folder.

3. Choose the **AdventureWorksDM** database (created within the *Getting ready* section previously mentioned) and expand the `Roles` folder.

If in case you are reading this recipe directly without the going through the previous recipes, you can create the necessary roles as per the _Creating security roles (Intermediate)_ recipe.

4. Right-click on the role (here I have selected the **DBIA_Reader** role) to choose **Role Properties**.

5. Click on **Dimension Custom Data Access** within the **Role Properties** page, choose the selective dimension in the dimension list (as shown in the following screenshot):

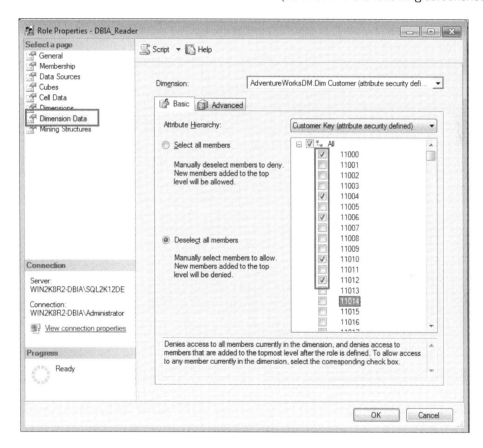

 The previous steps will present the opportunity to grant access permissions to selective members by clicking on the **Deselect all members** radio button.

6. The preceding step will enable the key ingredient for our recipe: setting the **IsAllowed** property to **True**.

7. To cross-check, you can select the **Advanced** tab that presents the list of dimensions in the **Allowed member set** window (see the following screenshot):

8. Here is the trick, to grant access for all the members you can select the **Select all members** radio button.

The preceding steps complete the initial process in granting *partial* access restrictions on selective dimensions. Now let us continue with the steps to give a database role access as *full* permissions to a member in a dimension:

1. Let us continue on the same SQL Server Management Studio and the selected Analysis Services instance.

2. Choose the **AdventureWorksDM** database (created within the *Getting ready* section previously mentioned) and expand the Roles folder.

 If you are reading this recipe directly without the previous recipes, you can create the necessary roles as per the *Creating security roles (Intermediate)* recipe.

3. Right-click on the role (here I have selected the **DBIA_Processor** role) to choose **Role Properties**.

4. Click on **Dimension Custom Data Access** within the **Role Properties** page, choose the **Select all members** radio button, which will allow access to all members currently in the dimension (as shown in the following screenshot).

 You may have observed from the preceding screenshot that not all the members were selected!

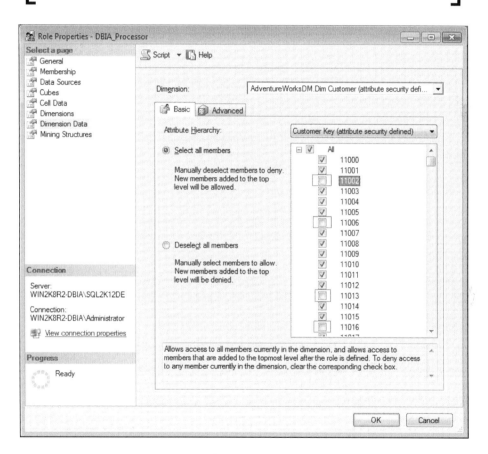

5. The reason behind selective members, shown in the screenshot, is to show how to deny a certain member set access to this particular database role (**DBIA_Processor**).

As a best practice, you can also choose to script the previous actions to an XML file, which can be executed on the preproduction (UAT) environment. This will keep the relevant object permissions intact.

6. Once the defined steps are followed, click on **OK** to complete the process.

How it works...

The previous steps are self-explanatory on granting necessary access restrictions on dimensions and defining default members.

The access restrictions on the dimensions can be controlled by using the database roles for the relevant members within that dimension. By using a database role, we can choose whether the members have permission to view or update dimension members within that database dimension. Further within a particular dimension to which a specific database role has been granted rights as FULL, that role can be granted permission to view or update specific dimension members only instead of all dimension members.

Let us talk about higher level permissions, such as a database role with permissions to access a cube. In such cases, the access permissions to dimensions in that cube are inherited from the permissions that are set on the dimension within a particular cube. The default structure of access restrictions is controlled from the database role that has access to all the members of all dimension attributes in a cube to which they have relevant access level.

The permissions are controlled by two properties, which are set to **AllowedSet** and **DeniedSet**. We can set the members in any of these attributes to which the role members have access rather than all of the members of the attributed hierarchy.

The **AllowedSet** property uses MDX that will determine which attribute members can be viewed by the database role. The set can include no members (the default), all members, or some attribute members. In case we allow access to an attribute and do not define any members of the allowed set, access to all members is granted. As a best practice, it is essential to outline specific attribute members added after the allowed set is defined.

Similarly, the **DeniedSet** property contains only a specific set of attribute members. In such cases, the database role is denied access only to those specific members. The definition of a denied set will affect the accessibility of attributed members that are added after the denied set is defined.

More information – section 1

As we have seen with access permissions on the dimension level, more to do with cell data is covered in the *Securing data at the cell level (Intermediate)* recipe.

Managing security surrounding an Analysis Services instance is quite possible by granting relevant permissions to the user roles and database roles. The security group can handle the users, members, and hierarchies in order to access the data from the cube.

Security management on the instance level and cube layers was covered in the previous recipe in the book; now we will dive into cell data specifics to manage the overall security efficiently.

In the series of recipes in this chapter we will highlight the importance of tools and tricks of the trade that will help to secure the data warehouse platform by providing necessary security to cube data. Not only the tools and tricks, we will also cook up recipes that drill down to the layers where they are essential when it comes to delivering diversified data for end users.

These recipes will also demonstrate the essential tools that can help to accomplish security management:

- ▸ How we can secure data at the cell level
- ▸ How we can prevent a process from reading/accessing certain cell data
- ▸ Managing user access privileges on cubes

Securing data at the cell level (Intermediate)

A bit of background on leaf members and non-leaf members is necessary to know how the data is managed at cell level.

The cell value in a cube can be obtained in multiple ways; it can be directly retrieved from the fact table of the cube. The identification of a cell value and its members is leaf members that have no child members or hierarchy that reference a single record in a dimension table.

Further on this cell can be identified by using non-leaf members, members that have one or more child members. The cell value is derived (typically) from the aggregation of child members.

Getting ready

The following prerequisite is essential for our recipe to continue the recipe:

- SQL Server 2012 Management Studio (SSMS).
- The AdventureWorks2012 database. We can obtain the necessary database files and database product samples from SQL Server Database Product Samples landing page (http://msftdbprodsamples.codeplex.com/releases/view/55330).

 These sample databases cannot be installed on any version of SQL Server other than SQL Server 2012 RTM or higher.

- Ensure you install the databases to your specified 2012 version instance.
- For this book I have created a new OLAP database using the AdventureWorksDM. xmla file.

 Also, ensure that the user who is granting permissions is a member of Analysis Services server role or member of Analysis Services database role that has Administrator permissions.

How to do it...

The following steps are continued from the previous recipe, but I believe
it is necessary to reiterate them from the beginning. Hence, this recipe's steps are listed
as follows:

1. Start the SQL Server Management Studio and connect to the SQL Server 2012
   Analysis Services instance.

2. Expand the `Databases` folder.

3. Choose the **AdventureWorksDM** database (created within the *Getting ready* section
   as previously mentioned) and expand the `Roles` folder.

> If you are reading this recipe directly without the previous recipes,
> you can create the necessary roles as per the *Creating security
> roles* (Intermediate) recipe.

4. Right-click on the role (here I have selected the **DBIA_Processor** role) to choose
   Role Properties.

5. Click on **Cell Data** on the **Select a page** option to present a relevant permissions list.

> In some cases, if you have observed that there is no option available
> in the **Cube** drop-down list in the **Cell Data** option, ensure you check
> that the relevant cube is set with appropriate **Access** and **Local
> Cube/Drillthrough** options by choosing the **Cubes** option on
> the left-hand side on **Select a page**.

Refer to the following screenshot:

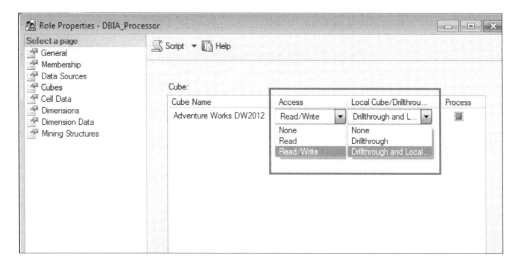

Now let us continue with the **Cell Data** options:

1. Click on **Cell Data** in the **Select a page** option to present a relevant permissions list.

2. Select the appropriate cube from the drop-down list; here I have selected the **Adventure Works DW2012** cube.

3. Choose the **Enable read permissions** option and then click on the **Edit MDX** button. You will be presented with the **MDX Builder** screen. Then, choose the presented **Metadata measure** value to grant this permission.

4. Similarly, for the **Enable read-contingent permissions** option, follow the previous step.

5. Finally, click on the **Enable read/write permissions** option.

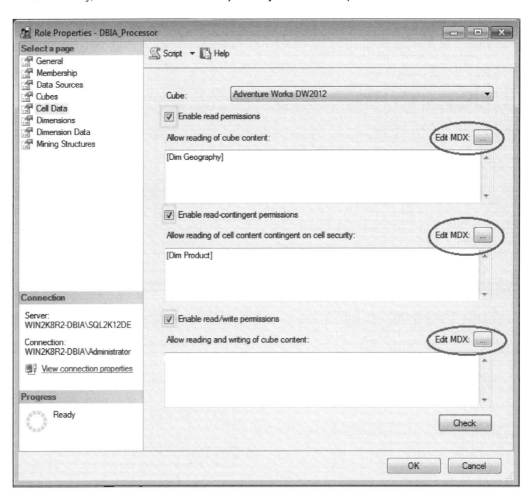

6. As a final check, either we can click on the **Check** button or the **OK** button, which will check whether valid syntax is parsed from the MDX expressions previously mentioned.

7. If there are any syntax errors, you can fix them by choosing the relevant **Edit MDX** button to correct.

This completes the steps to secure the data at the cell level using a defined role in the Analysis Services database.

How it works...

There are a few guidelines and some contextual information that will help us understand how we can best secure the data in a cell.

Nevertheless, whether the database role has read, read-contingent, or read/write permissions to the cell data, we need to ensure that we are granting permissions to derived cells correctly. By default, a derived cell obtains the relevant data from the other cells. So, the appropriate database role has the required permissions to the derived cell but not to the cells from which the derived cell obtain its values.

Irrespective of the database role, whether the members have read or write permissions on some or all the cells within a cube, the members of the database role have no permissions to view any cube data. Once the denied permissions on certain dimensions are effective, the cell level security cannot expand the rights of the database role members to include cell members from that dimension.

The blank expression within the relevant box will have no effect in spite of clicking on **Enable read/write permissions**. How this is effective is discussed in the following recipe.

Preventing read/access to cell data (Intermediate)

By default, if the database role has granted permissions on a cube, the role members have access to view all cell data. In order to limit the cell data access within the cube or dimension, we must explicitly restrict cell access.

For the specific dimension members, it is possible to limit the access; to grant relevant access we can use MDX to define a range of cells with the required permissions such as read, read-contingent, or read/write.

 The prerequisite for this recipe can be obtained from the *Getting ready* section in the *Designing and creating security roles in an OLAP database* recipe.

How to do it...

Perform the following steps:

1. Start the SQL Server Management Studio and connect to the SQL Server 2012 Analysis Services instance.

2. Expand the `Databases` folder.

3. Choose the **AdventureWorksDM** database (created within the *Getting ready* section previously mentioned) and expand the `Roles` folder.

 If you are reading this recipe directly without the previous recipes, you can create the necessary roles as per the *Creating security roles* (Intermediate) recipe.

4. Right-click on the role (here I have selected the **DBIA_Processor** role) to choose **Role Properties**.

5. Click on **Cell Data** in the **Select a page** option to be presented with a relevant permissions list.

 In some cases, if you have observed that there is no option available in the **Cube** drop-down list in the **Cell Data** option, ensure you check that the relevant cube is set with the appropriate **Access** and **Local Cube/Drillthrough** options by choosing the **Cubes** option on the left-hand side under **Select a page**.

6. Refer to the following screenshot:

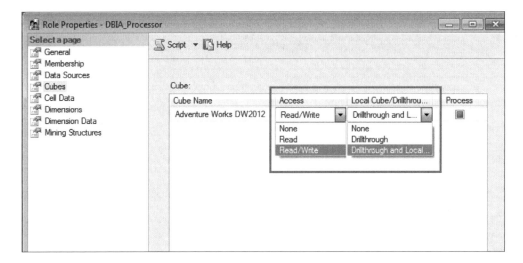

Now let us continue with the **Cell Data** options:

1. Click on **Cell Data** in the **Select a page** option to be presented with a relevant permissions list.

2. Select the appropriate cube from the drop-down list; here I have selected the **Adventure Works DW2012** cube.

3. Choose the **Enable read-contingent permissions** option and then click on the **Edit MDX** button. You will be presented with the **MDX Builder** screen. Then, choose the presented **Metadata** to grant this permission.

4. Similarly, for the **Enable read-contingent permissions** and the **Enable read/write permissions** options, perform the previous step:

 As shown in the following screenshot, choose the **[Dim Product]** measure for read-contingent permissions and the **[Dim Customer]** measure for the read/write permissions option.

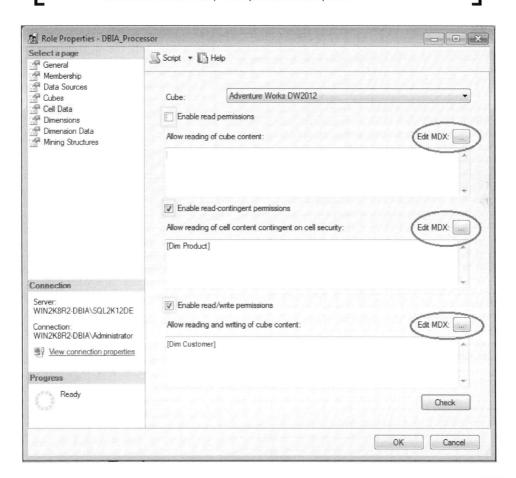

5. As a final check, either we can click on the **Check** button or the **OK** button, which will check whether the valid syntax is parsed from the previous MDX expressions.

6. If there are any syntax errors, you can fix them by choosing the relevant **Edit MDX** button to correct.

This completes the steps to prevent access to certain cell data using a defined role in the Analysis Services database.

How it works...

As we discussed in the previous recipe, irrespective of a database role with read or read-contingent permission to the cell data, there are certain steps that we have followed in this recipe to restrict the access to certain cell data and measures.

From the steps mentioned, we have selected the **[Dim Product]** measure for the read-contingent permission and the **[Dim Customer]** measure for the read/write permissions. In this case, the **DBIA_Processor** role has permissions for the cells of the product measure assigned as read-contingent that will allow reading of cell content contingent on cell security. This identifies the cells to which the database role has allocated permissions as per the steps. These measures are visible to the database role; however, the role does not have permissions to write on cells in product measure.

Just a note on how read-contingent permission works; with any cell that is specified as read-contingent, to which a database role has been assigned, this permission is only viewable if one of the following conditions is met:

▶ The read-contingent permissions are not derived from other cells

▶ The cells with read-contingent permissions are derived from the other cells; however, the database role has read permission on all the cells from which the cell was derived

The access permission for a specific database role cannot exceed the permissions that are granted to a database role on the entire cube. Also, access to certain cell databases does not give access to the dimension data. Access is granted to the dimension attributes to which the database role has access, but it cannot extend access to the dimension attributes to which the database role does not have access.

As we have seen in the previous steps, the MDX is necessary to allow that database role to contain relevant permissions. If the default allowed set is empty, the corresponding database role will be checked against permissions and no data will be allowed from the cell due to the empty set.

Managing user-access privileges on a cube (Advanced)

The user-access privilege is necessary to set up the production environment and make sure data access is not compromised. Once the design and implementation of a cube are finalized, the build and deployment are the next step. This is where we need to ensure that the cube will be processed without any errors, so testing is essential.

The opportunity to generate cube data access is determined by the settings in the cube role. Once the database role is defined with the privileges, the users and groups members of that role will have privileges in the Analysis Services objects associated with them.

In a SQL Server Analysis Services instance, the database role has no permissions to view any cubes (data) in the database; using the right method in granting user-access within a database role will enable the read or read/write permissions to a cube. In this recipe we will look into the user-access privileges on the cube.

The prerequisite for this recipe can be obtained from the *Getting ready* section from the *Designing and creating security roles in an OLAP database* recipe.

How to do it...

Perform the following steps:

1. Start SQL Server Management Studio and connect to the SQL Server 2012 Analysis Services instance.

2. Expand the Databases folder.

3. Choose the **AdventureWorksDM** database (created in the *Getting ready* section previously mentioned) and expand the Roles folder.

If you are reading this recipe directly without the previous recipes, you can create the necessary roles as per the *Creating security roles (Intermediate)* recipe.

4. Right-click on the role (here I have selected the **DBIA_Processor** and **DBIA_User** roles) to choose **Role Properties**.

5. Click on **Membership** in the **Select a page** option to **Specify the users and groups for this role**.

6. Click on the **Add** button to be presented with **Select Users or Groups** on the domain. Here I have selected the **DBIA_User** role for this step.

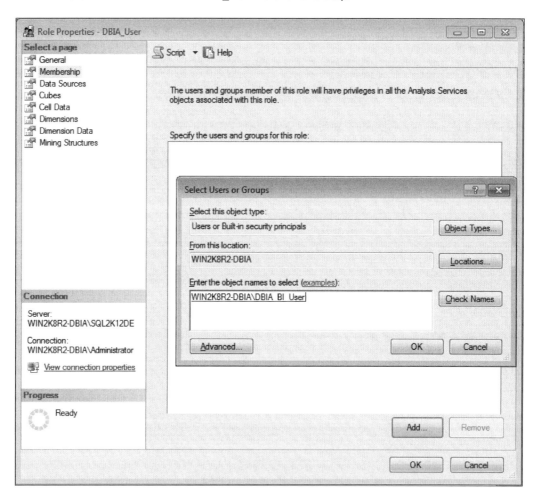

7. Click on the **OK** button to affect the relevant changes.

If you are not sure about domain names\login names, click on **Advanced** and **Find Now** to be presented with **Search results** for login names and user groups. To display **Groups**, click on **Object Types** and then select the types of objects you want to find and ensure **Groups** is selected.

As the previous steps are defined for the **DBIA_User** role, now I have chosen two logins and one Windows group to grant privilege for the **DBIA_Processor** database role.

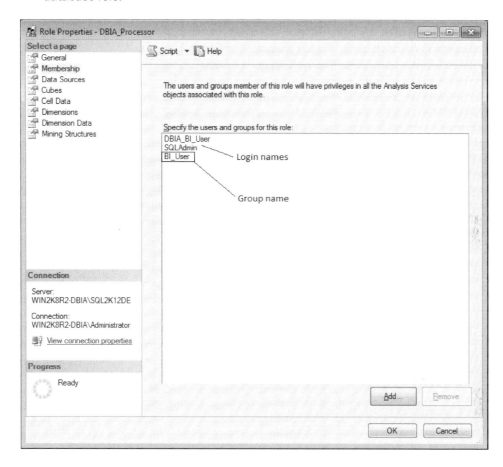

8. Click on the **OK** button to affect the relevant changes.

How it works...

As we have observed, with most recipes a database role provides all the necessary steps to enable the cube access within that **Analysis Services** (**AS**) instance.

Irrespective of the default settings for a database role, the privileges can be assigned to any cube (such as virtual or linked cubes) in the AS database. The recipe steps will grant the specified end users or groups in the database role access to the cube.

By default, the database role will not specify any restriction for the end users in the cube and a certain database role can view all members in the associated cube.

By design the end users in a cube role will be able to view all cells in the associated cube.

When the cube is set with write-enables, and also the role has been granted read/write access to the cube, the end users will be able to update the cube cells. In order to specify certain privileges for each cell, the security process will set relevant steps to define the access.

The security administration comprises many layers to handle, and at the same time continues industry best practices without any compromise. In these following recipes, we will highlight a definitive reference for important aspects of cube security processes by mirroring a quick reference on how best SQL Server 2012 BI features can help to accomplish goals.

Managing security roles for processing (Intermediate)

A user can be part of one or more roles in an Analysis Services database; the process to grant permissions across these roles is additive.

The **SQL Server Analysis Services** (**SSAS**) security is managed using roles, and the same is true for the AS database objects and data. By default, SIDs of Windows users and groups will have specific rights and permissions.

Again by default, the SSAS instance uses Windows Only authentication and no other authentication type. Within the Analysis Services there are two types of roles: server and database roles.

The server role is a fixed role that provides administrator access on the instance level. Similarly, the database role is defined by the administrators for access control to objects and data, which can be defined as read, read-contingent, or read/write purpose.

 The prerequisite for this recipe can be obtained from the *Getting ready* section of the *Designing and creating security roles in an OLAP database* recipe.

How to do it...

Perform the following steps:

1. Start SQL Server Management Studio and connect to the SQL Server 2012 Analysis Services (SSAS) instance.

2. Right-click on the SSAS instance and choose **Properties** to open the **Analysis Server Properties** page.

3. Choose the **Security** option from the **Select a Page** pane that will present a list of server administrators as shown in the following screenshot:

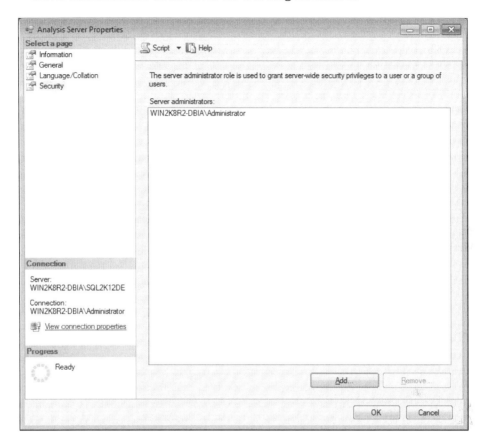

 As we observe the privileges on the server level, we can click on the **Add...** button to add the required users or groups to grant access on a server wide basis.

Now let us work on the database level security settings that will dictate the data source security information.

1. Expand the Databases folder, right-click on the **AdventureWorksDM** database, and then choose **Properties**.

 The default security settings on any SSAS instance are set as ImpersonateCurrentUser.

2. To change the **Data Source Impersonation Info** setting, click on the button with three dots; the **Impersonation Information** page will be displayed. As per the default settings, the radio button selection is set on **Use the credentials of the current user**.

3. For this recipe let us choose the **Use the service account** option.

4. Step 3 will bring about the changes immediately without having to restart the SSAS instance by changing the **Data Source Impersonation Info** setting to **ImpersonateServiceAccount**.

5. Click on **OK** to apply the changes on the **AdventureWorksDM** database.

How it works...

The relevant Analysis Services instance properties for the security page are used to specify the Windows users and groups included as members of the server administrator role for that instance.

The appropriate options at this level are to add or remove the NT Users and Groups, in order to enable them as server administrators. This means that the specified groups and users will have the highest privilege to perform any administrative action on the instance level. This will help to perform server-level administrative functions using the **SQL Server Management Studio** (**SSMS**) or **SQL Server Data Tools** (**SSDT**) that includes the database's creation or setting server level properties, and can be used for the programmatically administrative functions using **Analysis Management Objects** (**AMO**).

This server role cannot be deleted, permissions cannot be added or removed, and the specified user on this role is not an administrator for the instance of Analysis Services.

However, when it comes to the database level, the database properties dialog box will help us set the properties of a database. The data source impersonation information is the key factor to set for a relevant user to have the required privilege on a database-wide basis. This action specifies the default user credentials used to connect to data sources.

The impersonation options here will be specific to a Windows username (with password) service account, using credentials of the current user used to connect to the SSAS instance or default.

The database will be created as a separate object within the AS database and will only be applicable to the database in which that role is created. The permissions for this role may allow members to access or administer the database, in addition to to default access to objects and data.

By default, each permission has one or more access rights associated within that database, which in turn gives the permission finer control over access to that specified object in the database.

Data source and access control on cubes (Advanced)

The source is the key for any data, irrespective of cube or database. In this book the remaining areas within cube security are data sources and cube access. In this recipe we will go through the key aspects on how access control can affect the data sources and dimension data that are included in the cube.

Within the Analysis Services, data marts have multiple data sources and these types are not treated in the same way. When the cube is processed for query purposes, the key content of a right data type will help the results to return faster.

Cube processing also involves dimensions that will accept queries to the relational database in order to retrieve key information based on the queries. Keep in mind that not all the queries are simple SELECT queries or get a single dataset. There are multiple nested-complex queries. So, the data sources are always an important layer in the cube to set up the right level of data flow.

Here the permission is a key ingredient to access the data source, and it depends on the type of data that is being used and the security setup. As we have reiterated in the previous recipes, Analysis Services only uses Windows authentication to connect; it is one of the best ways to secure the data when OLAP is involved.

The account permissions for the SSAS service account will have the necessary access control on tables and views (virtual tables) with sufficient levels of read permissions. As we have worked out from the previous recipes, impersonal information is important to set up the right level of data access.

In this recipe we will look at the important steps used in order to secure a data source and right level of access on cubes.

 The prerequisite for this recipe can be obtained from the *Getting ready* section of the *Designing and creating security roles in an OLAP database* recipe.

How to do it...

Perform the following steps:

1. Start SQL Server Management Studio and connect to the SQL Server 2012 Analysis Services (SSAS) instance.

2. Expand the Databases folder.

3. Choose the **AdventureWorksDM** database (created in the *Getting ready* section previously mentioned) and expand the `Roles` folder.

 If you are reading this recipe directly without the previous recipes, you can create the necessary roles as per the *Creating security roles (Intermediate)* recipe.

4. Right-click on the role (here I have selected the **DBIA_Processor** role, and later the **DBIA_User** role) to choose **Role Properties**.

5. Select **Data Sources** from the **Select a page** pane that will show the **Adventure Works DW2012** information.

6. Click on the drop-down option on the **Access** column and select **Read** to enable the read access to the data source. Click on **OK** to bring about the new changes:

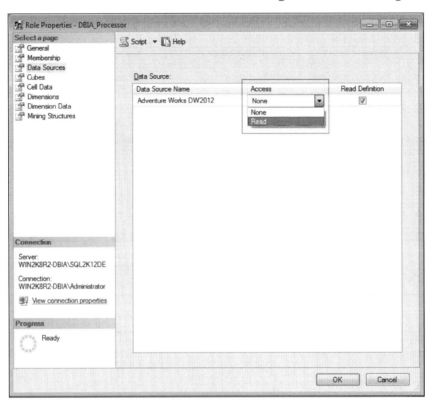

 For the **DBIA_User** role I would like to leave the default setting for **Access** as **None** under the **Data Sources** option.

We have completed the recipe steps for the data source now we will work out the cubes access steps. Start the process from step 4 from the previous steps:

1. Right-click on the role (here I have selected the **DBIA_Processor** role, and later the **DBIA_User** role) to choose **Role Properties**.

2. Select **Cubes** from the **Select a page** pane that will show the cube-related permissions for this role on the Adventure Works DW2012 cube.

3. Select the **Read/Write** option from the **Access** column's drop-down list and the **Drillthrough and Local Cube** option under the **Local Cube/Drillthrough Access** column:

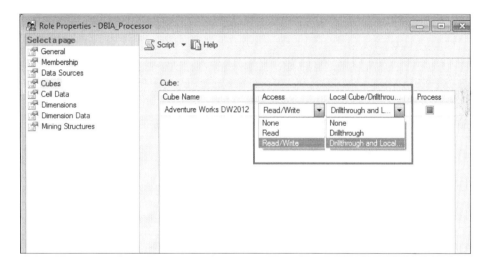

4. Click on **OK** to bring about the changes on the **Cubes** option, on the **Role Properties** page.

In the case of the **DBIA_User** role, I chose to apply **Read** for the **Access** column and **Drillthrough** for the option under the **Local Cube/Drillthrough Access** column.

How it works...

The steps carried out in this recipe take effect immediately without having to restart any services on the Analysis Services instance.

The data source name is applied from the database name, though we have an opportunity to change the name, which is not important at this point. On the screen, you will see the options to select the access level for the selected data source in this role.

The two options **None** and **Read** are self-explanatory. Using **None** will assure that users will be unable to access information from the data source. The **Read** option will enable users to read the information from that data source. The **Read Definition** option will help us to grant users to those who are in this role permission, for them to read metadata of the data source.

Now coming to the cubes permission, as we have seen the user must have the **Full Control** access for the specified SSAS instance, for any changes to take place for the role. The **Access** column will select the access level for the selected cube in this role.

The available options for this **Access** column levels are as follows:

> ▶ **None**: This will disallow any users from accessing the information from the cube
>
> ▶ **Read**: This will allow users to read the information
>
> ▶ **Read/Write**: This will allow users to read and write information to the cube

The **Local Cube/Drillthrough Access** column will enable the role to select the access level for the local cube or drillthrough functionality with the selected cube in this role.

The three options for this column are:

> ▶ **None**: This will disallow any access to the information from the cube
>
> ▶ **Drillthrough**: With this you will be able to use drillthrough functionality, but unable to create local cubes from the cube
>
> ▶ **Drillthrough and Local Cube**: We can use this to apply the complete drillthrough functionality and create local cubes from the cube

Finally, the **Process** column will grant users who are in this role the permission to process the selected cube.

 However, the **Process** option is selected but not available if the **Process database** option is selected on the **General** page of **Role Designer**.

Building a secure BI platform – the journey from SQL Server 2008 R2 to 2012 (Intermediate)

The Trustworthy Computing Initiative from Microsoft has made each of its products more secure and robust to stand out and empower the data needs in an efficient manner. Business Intelligence means data is presented normally to the users that will take full advantage of the data tools and existing security infrastructure to secure the data. The security framework in the corporate network must be robust to secure the BI environment.

When we talk about the Microsoft Business Intelligence stack, the three giants are SQL Server, SharePoint, and Office 365. In the last few years, Microsoft development teams have made great progress in securing the data platform by making secure designs. The data platform is the key perspective in safeguarding your data. The major security features include the following:

- Surface area reduction during the installation and disabled autostart of unwanted services

- Native encryption on the database

- User and schema separations

- Endpoint-based authentication with Group Policies on Active Directory

- Granular permissions in a least privileged environment

The major development since SharePoint 2007 is to prevent unauthorized users from viewing data, along with integrated AD authentication or forms authentication that provides a flexible security experience across the sites.

The new Office 365 platform provides end users with a flexible way of data presentation without having the need of other software and by simply using Microsoft Excel. The new features include analytics in analyzing data, ad hoc reporting with dashboards, and scorecards that fuel the powerful GUI frontend for business users.

SQL Server 2012 transports new changes on the Analysis Services foundational aspects that are divided into the modeling and server mode that gives an advantage of tools, tasks, and features that are available in the installed mode. The 2012 version provides a business intelligence semantic model that has three different approaches: tabular, multidimensional, and PowerPivot. These are mentioned in detail in the following list:

- A tabular model uses a relational modeling construct, such as tables and relationships, for data modeling that uses the **xVelocity** in-memory analytics engine for better performance for calculations and data storage.

- Multidimensional uses default OLAP modeling constructs used as cubes and dimensions, for data mining needs that use MOLAP, ROLAP, and HOLAP storage types.

- PowerPivot is a self-service BI solution that uses an analytical data model in Excel workbooks using **PowerPivot** as an Excel add-in. This model also uses the **xVelocity** method for the in-memory analytics engine for better performance for Excel and SharePoint. PowerPivot is very effective for data modeling and data rendering that will help workbook deployment on a server for a centralized and controlled data access, which requires SharePoint and Excel Services for better presentation to the end user.

In this recipe we will go through the important aspects in building a secure BI platform on the instance level along with enhancements incorporated in SQL Server since the transition from 2008 R2 to 2012.

The prerequisite for this recipe can be obtained from the *Getting ready* section of the *Designing and creating security roles in an OLAP database* recipe.

How to do it...

Perform the following steps:

1. Start SQL Server Management Studio and connect to the SQL Server 2012 Analysis Services (SSAS) instance.

2. Right-click on the SSAS instance. Choose **Properties** and click on the **General** option under the **Select a page** section.

3. By default the **Analysis Server Properties** window shows the default **Name** list for the chosen instance. Refer to the following screenshot:

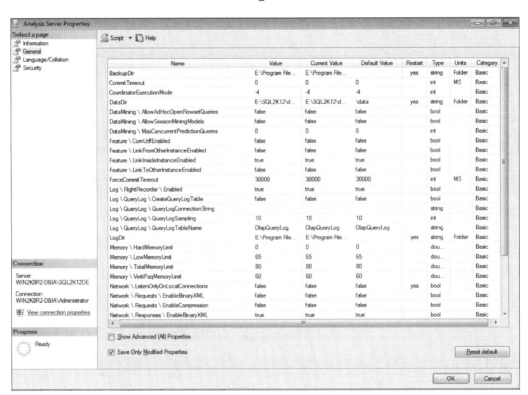

4. Click on **Show Advanced (All) Properties** that will change the **Name** list with all advanced options that are available for Analysis Services. Refer to the following screenshot:

The value **yes** within the **Restart** column indicates that any changes to these rows will require you to restart the specified SSAS instance.

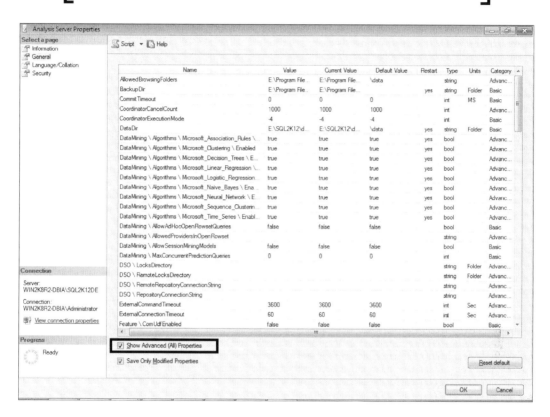

There are certain server properties that support tabular and multidimensional mode servers. Microsoft documentation suggests that, if SSAS is installed with PowerPivot for SharePoint, then you should make sure to use default values unless otherwise directed by a Microsoft product support engineer, on any occasion of a premier support case issue.

5. Specific to SQL Server 2008 R2, and in case of any specific troubleshooting on operational- or performance-based issues, refer to the *SQL Server 2008 R2 Analysis Services Operations Guide,* which can be downloaded from Microsoft Download center (or `http://download.microsoft.com/download/B/E/1/BE1AABB3-6ED8-4C3C-AF91-448AB733B1AF/SSASOpsGuide2008R2.docx`).

How it works...

The server property configuration is divided into multiple references. They are divided into multiple sections, and the following table explains these relevant SSAS configuration properties. (*Source: Microsoft SQL Server Documentation*).

The following topics explain the various Analysis Services configuration properties:

Topic	Description
General Properties	General properties are both basic and advanced properties, and include properties that define the data directory, backup directory, and other server behaviors.
Data Mining Properties	Data mining properties control which data mining algorithms are enabled and which are disabled. By default, all of the algorithms are enabled.
Feature Properties	Feature properties pertain to product features, most of them advanced, including properties that control links between server instances.
Filestore Properties	The filestore properties are for advanced use only. They include advanced memory management settings.
Lock Manager Properties	Lock manager properties define server behaviors pertaining to locking and timeouts. Most of these properties are for advanced use only.
Log Properties	Log properties controls whether, where, and how events are logged on the server. This includes error logging, exception logging, flight recorder, query logging, and traces.
Memory Properties	Memory properties control how the server uses memory. They are primarily for advanced use.
Network Properties	Network properties control server behavior pertaining to networking, including properties that control compression and binary XML. Most of these properties are for advanced use only.
OLAP Properties	OLAP properties control cube and dimension processing, lazy processing, data caching, and query behavior. These include both basic and advanced properties.

Topic	Description
Security Properties	The security section contains both basic and advanced properties that define access permissions. This includes settings pertaining to administrators and users.
Thread Pool Properties	Thread pool properties control how many threads the server creates. These are primarily advanced properties.

Securing key points in SSAS (Advanced)

Security and auditing are the primary concerns for a DBA, to secure business data that is stored in a cube, and the provision of end-to-end treatment of security configuration is beyond the scope of this book. However, the key points are referred to in this recipe to secure the cube data.

How to do it...

Perform the following steps:

1. Ensure that the SSAS instance is installed behind the firewall and the default port that the AS instance communicates with is **2383**.

2. To change the default port, scroll down to the **Port** row under the **Analysis Server? Properties** page and modify the **Current Value** column to a desired numbered value.

3. The SSAS instance can be set up to use HTTP to communicate with clients. In such cases, ensure that you open port 80 or port 443.

As a best practice ensure you open the assigned port number in the firewall for TCP/IP traffic. If the value is 0, the AS instance will use the 2382 port.

In order to connect to a named instance of SSAS, we can use the format of `[Server name{:[Port]`, in my case I have used **[WIN2K8R2-DBIA \SQL2K12DE:1453]**.

4. Bear in mind that you will need to open the port assigned here in your firewall for TCP/IP traffic. If you leave the default value at **0**, Analysis Services will use port **2382.**

To encrypt the cube transactions on the network, we can use the **Internet Protocol Security** (**IPSec**) method to achieve the encryption. Refer to this link for a step-by-step guide (`http://technet.microsoft.com/en-us/library/bb742429.aspx`).

5. Further, to ensure that all administrative data is encrypted:

    1. Under the **Analysis Server Properties** page, scroll down to **Security \ AdministrativeDataProtection\RequiredProtectionLevel** and ensure the value is set to **1**. Do not allow either 0 or 2, which is a lower level of security having no encryption for data transmission.

    2. Under the **Analysis Server Properties** page, scroll down to **Security \ DataProtection RequiredProtectionLevel** and ensure the value is set to **1**. Do not allow either **0** or **2**, which is a lower level of security having no encryption for data transmission.

    3. Under the **Analysis Server Properties** page, scroll down to **Network \ Request \EnableCompression** and ensure the value is set to **True**. The **EnableCompression** value is shown under the **Network \ Request a**nd **Network Responses** row.

How it works...

As we have followed the necessary steps to secure the BI platform, this section will explain the key points about why it is essential.

The best option to secure the cube data is to encrypt the filesystem used to store cubes. The SSAS service is executed using the `msmdsrv.exe` executable file that runs in the operating system. Every instance of SSAS is independent of each other on the same Windows server, having its own configuration settings stored under the `msmdsrv.ini` file. Any configuration changes for each instance, such as permissions, ports, file storage, server mode properties, and startup accounts, are different and can be configured separately.

The storage and memory architecture has been enhanced and redefined in the 2012 version.

Microsoft documentation states that:

> *A server that runs in multidimensional mode uses the resource management layer that was built for multidimensional cube databases and data mining models. In contrast, Tabular server mode uses the xVelocity in-memory analytics engine (VertiPaq) and data compression to aggregate data as it is requested.*

 Based on the configuration settings, each instance of Analysis Services runs either tabular or multidimensional databases, but not both. And the server mode property is best to determine which type of database runs on the instance.

The server mode can be set up during the installation, and in order to run multiple modes on the same server we can install SSAS as multiple instances. As a general rule, most administrative tasks you must perform do not vary by mode. As an Analysis Services system administrator, you can use the same procedures and scripts to manage any Analysis Services instance on your network regardless of how it was installed.

If you have configured Analysis Services to communicate over HTTP, the communication can be secured using the SSL protocol. However, be aware that you may have to acquire a certificate to use SSL encryption over public networks. Also, note that SSL encryption normally uses port 443, and not port 80, to communicate. This difference may require changes in the firewall configuration.

Using the HTTP protocol also allows you to run secured lines to parties outside the corporate network—for example, in an extranet setup.

More information – section 1

As we have seen, when it comes to managing SSAS instance configuration using the GUI options, the instance configuration can be managed using the `.ini` file from the specified instance. Let us work out the steps as follows:

1. On the server, where the SSAS Service instance is installed, open Windows Explorer to verify the location of Analysis Services program files or search for the `msmdsrv.ini` file.

 When SSAS is installed as the default instance, the aforementioned file can be found in the `%\Program Files\ Microsoft SQL Server\MSAS11.MSSQLSERVER\OLAP\ Config` folder. Ensure that the `msmdsrv.ini` file is backed up before performing any changes.

2. Open the file using `notepad.exe` or any other text editor.

3. Ensure that you restart SQL Server Analysis Services (SSAS) once the file is modified and saved to bring about the new changes.

About Packt Publishing

Packt, pronounced 'packed', published its first book "*Mastering phpMyAdmin for Effective MySQL Management*" in April 2004 and subsequently continued to specialize in publishing highly focused books on specific technologies and solutions.

Our books and publications share the experiences of your fellow IT professionals in adapting and customizing today's systems, applications, and frameworks. Our solution based books give you the knowledge and power to customize the software and technologies you're using to get the job done. Packt books are more specific and less general than the IT books you have seen in the past. Our unique business model allows us to bring you more focused information, giving you more of what you need to know, and less of what you don't.

Packt is a modern, yet unique publishing company, which focuses on producing quality, cutting-edge books for communities of developers, administrators, and newbies alike. For more information, please visit our website: www.packtpub.com.

Writing for Packt

We welcome all inquiries from people who are interested in authoring. Book proposals should be sent to author@packtpub.com. If your book idea is still at an early stage and you would like to discuss it first before writing a formal book proposal, contact us; one of our commissioning editors will get in touch with you.

We're not just looking for published authors; if you have strong technical skills but no writing experience, our experienced editors can help you develop a writing career, or simply get some additional reward for your expertise.

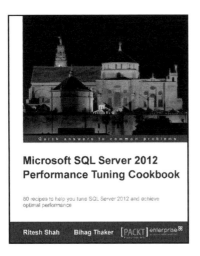

Microsoft SQL Server 2012 Performance Tuning Cookbook

ISBN: 978-1-849685-74-0   Paperback: 478 pages

80 recipes to help you tune SQL Server 2012 and archieve optimal performance

1. Learn about the performance tuning needs for SQL Server 2012 with this book and ebook

2. Diagnose problems when they arise and employ tricks to prevent them

3. Explore various aspects that affect performance by following the clear recipes

SQL Server 2012 with PowerShell V3 Cookbook

ISBN: 978-1-849686-46-4   Paperback: 634 pages

Increase your productivity as a DBA, developer, or IT Pro, by using PowerShell with SQL Server to simplify database management and automate repetitive, mundane tasks

1. Provides over a hundred practical recipes that utilize PowerShell to automate, integrate and simplify SQL Server tasks

2. Offers easy to follow, step-by-step guide to getting the most out of SQL Server and PowerShell

3. Covers numerous guidelines, tips, and explanations on how and when to use PowerShell cmdlets, WMI, SMO, .NET classes or other components

Please check **www.PacktPub.com** for information on our titles

Microsoft SQL Server 2012 Integration Services: An Expert Cookbook

ISBN: 978-1-849685-24-5   Paperback: 564 pages

Over 80 expert recipes to design, create, and deploy SSIS packages

1. Full of illustrations, diagrams, and tips with clear step-by-step instructions and real time examples

2. Master all transformations in SSIS and their usages with real-world scenarios

3. Learn to make SSIS packages re-startable and robust; and work with transactions

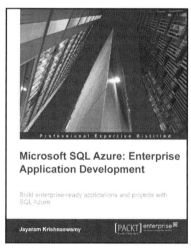

Microsoft SQL Azure Enterprise Application Development

ISBN: 978-1-849680-80-6   Paperback: 420 pages

Build enterprise-ready applications and projects with SQL Azure

1. Develop large scale enterprise applications using Microsoft SQL Azure

2. Understand how to use the various third party programs such as DB Artisan, RedGate, ToadSoft etc developed for SQL Azure

3. Master the exhaustive Data migration and Data Synchronization aspects of SQL Azure.

Please check **www.PacktPub.com** for information on our titles

Printed in Great Britain
by Amazon.co.uk, Ltd.,
Marston Gate.